UNUSUAL LiFE CYCLES OF

BIRDS

by Jaclyn Jaycox

CAPSTONE PRESS
a capstone imprint

Capstone Captivate is published by Capstone Press, an imprint of Capstone.
1710 Roe Crest Drive
North Mankato, Minnesota 56003
www.capstonepub.com

Library of Congress Cataloging-in-Publication Data is available on the Library of Congress website.
ISBN: 978-1-4966-9557-4 (hardcover)
ISBN: 978-1-4966-9701-1 (paperback)
ISBN: 978-1-9771-5522-1 (eBook PDF)

Summary: Have you ever heard of a bird that lays its eggs on the ground instead of in a nest? What about a bird that lays eggs in other birds' nests? Young readers will learn all about killdeers, cuckoo birds, and other birds with unusual life cycles.

Image Credits
Alamy/ART Collection, 25; Shutterstock: Ben Petcharapiracht, 15, Cheryl E. Davis, 5, Chris Watson, 11, cynoclub, cover, Dan Bagur, 29, DisaAnna, 7, Dziewul, 9, John Navajo, 19, JT Platt, 13, Michael Thaler, 27, Mohamad halid, 21, Riza Marion, 23, Vishnevskiy Vasily, 17

Design elements: Shutterstock: emEF, Max Krasnov

Editorial Credits
Editor: Gena Chester; Designer: Bobbie Nuytten; Media Researcher: Kelly Garvin; Production Specialist: Laura Manthe

All internet sites appearing in back matter were available and accurate when this book was sent to press.

Words in **bold** are in the glossary.

Table of Contents

CHAPTER 1

Bird Life Cycle

Look out your window and up toward the sky. Can you see a bird soaring? Birds are found all around the world. There are about 18,000 different kinds of birds.

Most birds have the same life cycle. They begin life inside eggs. In spring, a female makes a nest out of sticks, leaves, mud, and feathers. She lays between two and six eggs. Some kinds of birds lay only one egg. Some lay more than six. The female sits on the eggs to keep them warm. The male helps guard the nest. He brings food back for the female. Soon the baby birds hatch. Most have no feathers and can't open their eyes. Their parents bring them food and keep them safe and warm.

Baby robins wait for food.

Baby birds grow quickly. They start to sprout fuzzy feathers. They learn to stand on their feet. Their parents feed and care for them. Young birds leave the nest. At first, they cannot fly. They walk, hop, and flutter around on the ground. They stay near their parents. They learn how to find food. Their wings get stronger. Soon they learn how to fly. When they have finished growing, they are adults. They will **mate** and lay eggs of their own.

This is the life cycle many birds go through. But there are a few that do things a bit differently. Some birds can "talk" to their parents from inside the egg. Others lay eggs in interesting places. And some don't raise their babies. Let's take a look at birds with unusual life cycles.

A BIRD'S LIFE CYCLE

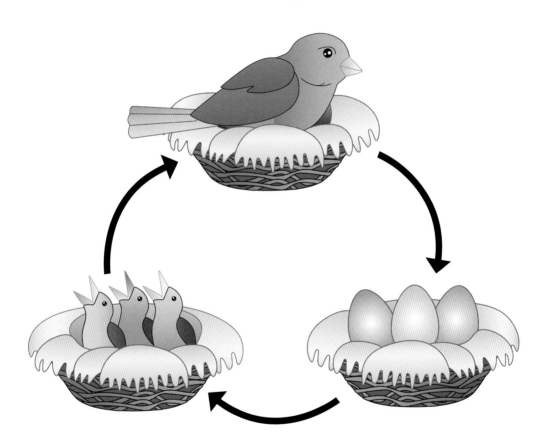

CHAPTER 2

Strange Nests

Nests are places for birds to lay their eggs. They raise their babies there. They build them each year using lots of different things. Nests can be found on tree branches, cliffs, and even on the ground. But some birds don't build nests like others do. In fact, some don't build nests at all!

Budgies

Instead of a nest, budgies lay their eggs in hollow spaces in trees called **cavities**. Budgies live in groups called **flocks**. Many of these birds will lay their eggs in the same tree. Staying in groups helps protect them from **predators** such as snakes and larger birds. There are lots of eyes to keep a lookout for danger. They call out to each other to give warning if trouble is near.

a budgie sitting in its nest

Many birds **breed** at the same time each year. But the breeding season for budgies is different. They only lay eggs when there is enough food and water available. They live in Australia. It is one of the driest places in the world. It also gets very hot in the summer. Even after a heavy rain, the heat can dry up a water hole quickly. Budgies must **migrate** to find food and water.

Budgies have been around for 5 million years. Their breeding activity helps them survive.

Fact!

Budgies have a small bump above their beaks. If the bump is blue, the budgie is a male. If it is brown, it's a female budgie.

A flock of budgies flies over a watering hole in Australia to drink.

Hornbills

Hornbills are another kind of bird that nests inside trees. They can be found in Africa and Southeast Asia. If there are not enough empty tree cavities, female hornbills will fight each other for them. Sometimes they find a cavity with another animal already living in it. They will fight with other birds, snakes, or lizards to take over their home.

Once they are inside, they work on covering up the hole. A male brings mud to build a wall over the hole. The male and female work together until the hole is completely covered, except for a small slit. The female will use this small opening to get food from the male. The small opening keeps her safe from predators. Monkeys, snakes, and large birds eat eggs and young hornbills.

Fact!

Red-cockaded woodpeckers are cavity nesters too. But they make their own holes in trees. It can take up to six years for one to finish its hole!

a hornbill in its nest

Female hornbills lay two to six eggs. Females depend on males to bring them food. After the eggs hatch, a male can make up to 70 trips to the nest each day! Hornbills eat bugs, berries, seeds, and small lizards.

Some types of hornbills spend up to five months inside the cavity with their young. Then the chicks are ready to fly. The mother and young break out of the nest.

Other kinds of hornbills leave when the babies are half grown. The young are sealed back up in the hole. The female helps the male with feedings. After about two to three months, the chicks' voices change. The parents stop bringing them food. The young hornbills start chipping away at the mud wall until they break out.

young hornbills leaving the nest for the first time

CHAPTER 3
On Their Own

Cuckoos

Many kinds of birds take care of their babies. They feed them and keep them safe until they are ready to leave the nest. But this is not the case for cuckoos.

Cuckoos do not make nests. Instead, they find **host** nests. The cuckoo will wait until another female bird leaves her nest of eggs. Before she can return, the cuckoo will lay an egg in the nest. Then the cuckoo takes one of the other eggs from the nest. She quickly flies away before the host returns. The cuckoo egg **mimics** what the other eggs in the nest look like. A female cuckoo can lay up to 25 eggs in other birds' nests each year. She never sees them again.

A cuckoo egg (left) mimics the color and spots of warbler eggs.

MASTER MIMICS

Cuckoos are masters of mimicry. They are able to trick more than 120 different kinds of birds into raising their young. Not only can their eggs fool other birds, but the adults can too. Cuckoos can mimic the sound of a predatory bird that scares other female birds from their nests. This gives cuckoos time to swoop in and switch the eggs.

The host bird has no idea one of the eggs is a cuckoo egg. She keeps the egg warm. Cuckoo eggs hatch after about 12 days. They usually hatch before the other eggs in the nest. The baby birds are as sneaky as their mothers. They will kick the other eggs out of the nest. This ensures their survival. They will get all the food from their host parents.

The host parents raise the baby as their own. They keep the cuckoo bird fed and safe. The young bird grows and grows. It is usually much larger than its host parents. But they don't notice. After about three weeks, the cuckoo is ready to leave the nest.

A robin feeds a cuckoo baby, which the robin thinks is its own.

Maleos

Maleos look similar to chickens. They have large legs and feet. Their strong legs are useful for making nests. They live in forests. But maleos make their nests on open, sandy beaches.

Maleos dig large holes about 3 feet (1 meter) deep. The female lays an egg in the hole. The egg is large. It is about five times bigger than a chicken egg. Then the male and female fill the hole with sand. Females lay up to 12 eggs over two to three months. Then they leave the eggs to survive on their own.

a maleo digging its nest on the beach

Maleo eggs are kept warm by the heat from the ground and sun. They can take up to three months to hatch. The babies must dig their way to the surface. It's a long journey for a newly hatched chick! It can take two days for the baby to make its way out of the sand.

Baby maleos have all their feathers. They are able to fly right away. After coming out of the sand, they must hide from predators. They run into the forest. Sometimes they immediately take off flying into a tree. Without help from their parents, they learn to find food and to fight off predators.

a baby maleo just getting out of the sand

CHAPTER 4

Smart Eggs

American White Pelicans

American white pelicans lay eggs between March and May each year. They make their nests on the ground. They nest in **colonies**. Females lay two eggs. Both parents help to keep the eggs warm. They take turns every few days. Instead of sitting on the eggs, they warm them under their webbed feet.

These eggs are special. Before they hatch, the young will squawk from inside their eggs. The noise tells the parents if the babies are too hot or too cold. This helps to keep the eggs healthy and ensures the chicks will hatch. After both are hatched, usually only one chick survives. The smaller baby pelican can't compete with the bigger one for food.

American white pelican eggs in their nest

MYSTERY HORN

Each breeding season, adult American white pelicans get flashy to attract mates. Their beaks and legs turn bright orange. They grow long hair on the backs of their heads. They also grow a mysterious orange horn on their bills. It falls off in May and grows back the next year. Scientists aren't sure what the purpose of the horn is. American whites are the only kind of pelican that grows a horn.

CHAPTER 5

Life at Sea

Puffins

Puffins are unique birds in many ways. They are much better swimmers than they are fliers. So they spend most of their lives floating and swimming in the ocean. They only come to land to breed.

Puffins mate for life. Each spring, they head to shore to lay their eggs. Mates use the same nesting area every year. They dig **burrows** in rocky cliffs. Inside the burrow, they make a nest out of grass and feathers. A female lays one egg. Both parents take turns keeping the egg warm. After about 40 days, it hatches. A baby puffin is called a puffling.

Fact!

Puffins are often called "clowns of the sea" because of their colorful beaks.

puffins entering their burrow

Both parents take turns feeding the puffling. They guard the burrow to keep the baby safe from predators. The puffling must stay clean. Getting dirty can ruin its waterproof feathers. Puffins even have a separate area in their burrow to poop.

After about one month, the parents head back to sea. The young puffin stays a little longer. After about a week it leaves the nest to find food. It takes off flying out to the ocean.

Puffins spend their first two to five years at sea. They learn to hunt for food on their own. They return to land. They are ready to find their mates and lay eggs at 5 to 6 years old.

a young puffin leaving its burrow

Glossary

breed (BREED)—to mate and produce young

burrow (BUR-oh)—a hole or tunnel used as a house

cavity (KAV-i-tee)—a hole

colony (KAH-luh-nee)—a large group of animals that live together in the same area

flock (FLAHK)—a group of the same kind of animal; members of flocks live, travel, and eat together

host (HOST)—an animal that another animal uses to survive

mate (MATE)—to join together to produce young; a mate is also the male or female partner of a pair of animals

migrate (MYE-grate)—to move from one place to another

mimic (MIM-ik)—to copy

predator (PRED-uh-tur)—an animal that hunts other animals for food

Read More

Allan, John. *Birds*. Cornwall, UK: Hungry Tomato Ltd., 2019.

Jacobson, Bray. *Bird Life Cycles*. New York: Gareth Stevens Publishing, 2018.

Myers, Maya. *National Geographic Readers: Puffins*. Washington, D.C.: National Geographic Kids, 2019.

Internet Sites

Animalia: American White Pelican
animalia.bio/american-white-pelican#:~:text=Fun%20 Facts%20for%20Kids&text=An%20American%20white%20 pelican%20is,to%20breathe%20through%20their%20beaks

Fort Wayne Children's Zoo: Silvery-Cheeked Hornbill
kidszoo.org/our-animals/silvery-cheeked-hornbill/

National Geographic Kids: Atlantic Puffin
kids.nationalgeographic.com/animals/birds/atlantic-puffin/

Index